The Bot in Bede

Written by
John Wood

Illustrated by
Beth Barnett

Neve is an athlete from the little town of Bede. This morning, Neve is skipping.

It is bright and still in Bede. But wait!
What is that on the hill?

It looks like a bot. There is clanking and clanging as the bot gets nearer.

A crowd forms. Neve the athlete picks flowers for the bot. Will the bot like them?

"These flowers are a mess," booms the bot. Pop! The bot deletes the flowers.

The bot can delete things! The crowd yelps in fright. What will it delete next?

"This food is a mess," booms the bot.
"I did my best," sniffs the cook.

The bot deletes the food. The crowd howl in fright and jump up and down.

"This art is a mess," booms the bot.
"That is not fair!" wails a man.

The bot deletes the art. The crowd bump into things as they run up and down.

"These fish are a mess," booms the bot. The fish look up at the bot.

The bot deletes the pond and the fish.
The crowd are afraid. What will be next?

"Quick!" yells a man. Neve and her chums run in.
"I am Steve," he tells them.

"The bot comes from my lab," sighs Steve. "It took me years to complete it."

"It had orders to clear up mess, but now it will not stop!" Steve tells the kids.

"Inventing bots is a bit extreme," mutters Neve. "Pick mess up like the rest of us!"

The kids have a plan.
"We must mess up the bot so it deletes itself!"

"We can chuck paint at it!"
The kids run along the concrete streets
to the shop.

They grab the paint and look for the bot.
It is evening now.

There is the bot, at the theme park. They creep after it, back to the town.

"We must help Bede," Neve tells them.
"We must get rid of this bot!"

The kids jump up with the paint tins.
"Now!" they yell.

But then they all slip on the street.
The paint splats and spills.

Paint coats the town from top to bottom.
It is a complete mess.

"This was a bad plan," groan the kids.
The bot turns and sees the mess.

Pop! The bot deletes the town. And that is the end of that.

The Bot in Bede

1)   What is the name of the town?

2)   What is the first thing that the bot deletes?

3)   What do the kids plan to use to mess up the bot?
     a) Rubbish
     b) Glitter
     c) Paint

4)   If you were going to invent a robot, what would your robot do?

5)   Can you think of a better plan to stop a robot that deletes everything?

©2022 **BookLife Publishing Ltd.**
King's Lynn, Norfolk PE30 4LS

ISBN 978-1-80155-063-5

The Bot in Bede
Written by John Wood
Illustrated by Beth Barnett

An Introduction to BookLife Readers...

Our Readers have been specifically created in line with the London Institute of Education's approach to book banding and are phonetically decodable and ordered to support each phase of the Letters and Sounds document.

Each book has been created to provide the best possible reading and learning experience. Our aim is to share our love of books with children, providing both emerging readers and prolific page-turners with beautiful books that are guaranteed to provoke interest and learning, regardless of ability.

BOOK BAND GRADED using the Institute of Education's approach to levelling.

PHONETICALLY DECODABLE supporting each phase of Letters and Sounds.

EXERCISES AND QUESTIONS to offer reinforcement and to ascertain comprehension.

BEAUTIFULLY ILLUSTRATED to inspire and provoke engagement, providing a variety of styles for the reader to enjoy whilst reading through the series.

AUTHOR INSIGHT:
JOHN WOOD

An incredibly creative and talented author, John Wood has written about 60 books for BookLife Publishing. Born in Warwickshire, he graduated with a BA in English Literature and English Language from De Montfort University. During his studies, he learned about literature, styles of language, linguistic relativism, and psycholinguistics, which is the study of the effects of language on the brain. Thanks to his learnings, John successfully uses words that captivate and resonate with children and that will be sure to make them retain information. His stories are entertaining, memorable, and extremely fun to read.

INTRO TO PHASE 5

/e_e/

This book introduces the phoneme /e_e/ and is a Blue+ Level 4+ book band.